MW01282700

In His Presence

Thirty Contemplations from Walking

with Jesus

Daniel Hamlin

I pray this book
blesses you!

Dan

To Jesus

I am astonished by Your extravagant grace.

Thank You for Your constant companionship and

unending love.

Day 1

Now the LORD said to Abram, "Go forth from your country…to the land which I will show you…" So Abram went forth as the LORD had spoken to him. From Genesis 12:1-4

Abraham was asked to do something that didn't make sense. He didn't have a well thought out plan or even a specific destination. But he knew what the Lord had spoken to him, and he knew he needed to obey. Sometimes the Lord asks us to do things that don't make sense to us. Those around us might think we're foolish, but if the Lord has spoken, we need to obey at all costs. Abraham's life is full of examples of this kind of obedience. He did not worry about every little detail—he simply obeyed God. His obedience was based on his personal relationship with the Lord. He had spent time with the Lord, and he had seen how God was always faithful in every circumstance. He trusted in the Lord; he trusted in who He had shown Himself to be. So in those difficult times, he could confidently obey in full assurance that God would be faithful. And just as God always proved to be faithful in Abraham's life, so He will always prove to be faithful in our lives.

Day 2

But on the night immediately following, the Lord stood at his side and said, "Take courage; for as you have solemnly witnessed to My cause at Jerusalem, so you must witness at Rome also."
Acts 23:11

The apostle Paul was a man full of the Spirit and of faith. Yet he was simply a man, and despite all his faith he still felt scared that night in the jail cell. There are times in our spiritual walks when we are all too aware of the dangers that lurk around us; we fear what our obedience to Christ might cost. It's at these times that our loving Jesus stands by our side and encourages us to take courage and not be fearful. He comforts us by letting us know that He has a plan for our lives and will not abandon us. In the loneliness of a jail cell the Lord appeared to Paul and stood by his side to encourage him, and He will do the same for all His children no matter the

circumstances.

Day 3

Philip went down to the city of Samaria and began proclaiming Christ to them. The crowds with one accord were giving attention to what was said by Philip, as they heard and saw the signs which he was performing.
So there was much rejoicing in that city.
Acts 8:5-6, 8

Philip was in the midst of a very fruitful time of ministry in Samaria when the Lord told him to leave and "go south to the road that descends from Jerusalem to Gaza" (Acts 8:26). The Bible tells us this was a desert road. In effect, the Lord had Philip leave a thriving ministry in Samaria to go to the desert. I'm sure Philip must have been wondering if the Lord knew what He was doing as he obediently set out toward the desert road. But Philip's obedience resulted in the salvation of a very influential man in the nation of Ethiopia. Like

ripples in a pond, the effect of Philip's obedience

spread far and wide. The same is true when we obey

the Lord. Though we might not understand from our

perspective, we can rest assured that He has a plan.

And our obedience ushers in His purposes in our

lives and often also in the lives of others.

Day 4

For the report of your obedience has reached to all; therefore I am rejoicing over you, but I want you to be wise in what is good and innocent in what is evil. The God of peace will soon crush Satan under your feet. The grace of our Lord Jesus be with you. Romans 16:19-20

Have you ever considered the magnitude of our obedience to Christ? Paul tells us here that it reaches to all. In other words, our obedience has an effect on the world. What a remarkable concept to grasp. In 1 Samuel 15: 22 we are told, "Behold, to obey is better than sacrifice…" There is something in the heart of God that is moved when His children willingly choose to obey Him. Our obedience allows God unhindered movement in our lives, thus allowing Him to move through us to carry out His purposes. It's His kingdom we want to advance, not our own, and our obedience partners us with Him in

advancing that eternal cause.

Day 5

…for I know whom I have believed and I am convinced that He is able to guard what I have entrusted to Him until that day.
2 Timothy 1:12b

In one of Paul's last earthly writings he discloses to us the root of his steadfastness. He didn't just believe in Jesus, he *knew* Him. It was this close relationship with Jesus that would sustain Paul in one of the loneliest times of his life. He goes on to say in his second letter to Timothy that when he was put on trial for the sake of the gospel, not one person stood by his side—all deserted him. It's sad to think that after all Paul had done, all the people he served and ministered to, not one of them stood by him in support. But it did not affect Paul in the least, for he says, "But the Lord stood with me and strengthened me…" (2 Timothy 4:17). Paul's steadfast faith resulted from his intimate relationship with Christ. All his needs were met in the person of Jesus, whether they were companionship, support, strength, or whatever else he needed in his life. He looked only to Jesus. And we can have the same type of relationship with Christ as Paul did. Jesus is eager to reveal Himself to those who desire to know Him.

Day 6

And David said, "The LORD who delivered me from
the paw of the lion and from the paw of the bear, He
will deliver me from the hand of this Philistine."
1 Samuel 17:37a

David was in the midst of a battle. The opposing
army was physically stronger, yet David was certain
he would not be defeated. He was positive the Lord
would grant him victory. As David prepared to go
to battle with the giant who was opposing the Lord
and His people, David remembered past occasions
when the Lord had delivered him from seemingly
certain death. It's important for us to remember
what the Lord has done in our lives—to recall the
faithfulness He has always shown us. In our times
of battle, when the enemy opposes us like an
overpowering giant, let us not forget that in Christ

we are more than conquerors. He will deliver us and grant us victory. Despite the giant's weapons and stature, it only took a sling and a stone for David to slay him. David's faith in the Lord made him triumphant in battle.

Day 7

So he went away and washed, and came back seeing. Therefore the neighbors, and those who previously saw him as a beggar, were saying, "Is not this the one who used to sit and beg?" The Jews then did not believe it of him, that he had been blind and had received sight… John 9:7b-8, 18a

This blind man who received sight used to sit and beg every day from his neighbors. Every day his neighbors had the chance to help him. Their inability to recognize him after he received his sight shows the amount of time they gave him while he was a beggar. The Messiah just performed a miracle in this man's life, and no one even recognized him. This shows how close we can be to Jesus's miraculous workings and yet still miss them if we aren't rightly related to Him. The fact that our Lord noticed this beggar while everyone else passed him by reminds us to notice those in our daily lives who might seem insignificant. The Lord wants to do a miracle in their lives just as he did with the blind beggar. No one is insignificant in our Savior's eyes.

Day 8

For judgment is without mercy to the one who has shown no mercy. Mercy triumphs over judgment. James 2:13

Never in all of history has this verse been manifested the way it was on the cross. I was reminded recently of the actual cause of Jesus's death. John tells us of the soldier piercing Jesus's side and how blood and water poured forth. Medicine has taught us that when blood and water build up like this, one of the causes can be the heart rupturing. So in a very real sense one could say Jesus died of a broken heart. It's this heart of mercy that the Lord desires to see in His children. We need to see people through the filter of mercy the way Christ does. Mercy certainly does triumph over judgment. For the doubting who would seek proof you need only look to the cross. It was on the cross

that mercy triumphed eternally over judgment.

Day 9

But supposing Him to have been in the company,
they went a day's journey, and sought Him among
their relatives and acquaintances. So when they did
not find Him, they returned to Jerusalem, seeking
Him.
Luke 2:44-45

This passage in Luke 2 about Jesus's parents
accidentally leaving Him in Jerusalem after they
had gone there to observe the Feast of the Passover
is an error we all might make. You see, His parents
had gone to do what they were supposed to. They
sincerely sought to honor the Lord. But in doing so
they unknowingly made the mistake we all are at
risk of making. They assumed that Jesus was in
their presence, instead of making it a point to make
sure they were in His presence (v. 44). When doing
service for the Lord, it's often easy to assume that

Jesus is in our presence. We lose sight of the whole purpose in serving the Lord—to be in His presence. "If anyone serves Me, let him follow Me; and where I am, there My servant will be also. If anyone serves Me, him my Father will honor." John 12:26

Day 10

"And the Angel of the LORD appeared to him and said to him, "The LORD is with you, you mighty man of valor!" Gideon said to Him, "O my lord, if the LORD is with us, why then has all this happened to us? And where are His miracles which our fathers told us about, saying, 'Did not the LORD bring us up from Egypt?'...Then the LORD turned to him and said, "Go in this might of yours, and you shall save Israel from the hand of the Midianites. Have I not sent you?" So he said to Him, "O my Lord..."
From Judges 6:12-15

In the original Hebrew we understand that Gideon's response to the Lord at the beginning of the conversation shows he clearly didn't know who was speaking to him. He addressed the Lord as though he were merely addressing another man (verse 13). He was so consumed by his current problems he was not looking for the Lord to show up. It's at these times, when trials overwhelm us, that we often lose sight of the Lord as we focus on the trial. It's also at these times that the Lord often wants to speak directly to us. And if we aren't looking to Him, we risk missing what He has for us. In verse 15 we see that Gideon realized who was speaking to him because this time when he addressed Him as Lord in the original Hebrew it was referring to God. His grumbling turned to a feeling of inadequacy, which turned to an attitude of worship. It's in this state of worship that the Lord desires us to be. It's here where the Lord can use the most unlikely of people to change history.

Day 11

For I determined to know nothing among you
except Jesus Christ, and Him crucified.
1 Corinthians 2:2

Of all the apostles, surely Paul had reason to boast.
He had been brought up with the highest of
education, had seen visions words couldn't
describe. At one point the Lord's anointing was so
strong on him that his handkerchiefs were sent to
the sick, and they were healed. And yet he boasted
of none of this. He did not rely on his qualifications;
he relied on Him, the one he knew. He knew Jesus
Christ. He knew Him who called him. Where is our
confidence? Is it in our qualifications, our talents, or
our visions? May our confidence be found only in
Jesus Christ and may we truly know Him.

Day 12

From that time Jesus began to preach and say,
"Repent, for the kingdom of heaven is at hand."
Matthew 4:17

When Jesus says "repent" in this verse, most of the
time it is thought He is simply saying, "Confess
your sins and stop sinning." It's often translated as
"to do a 180." These are both correct teachings, but
they only begin to give the full implication of what
Jesus was saying. When He says "repent," He is
saying in essence, "begin to think differently." Jesus
is saying heaven is within our grasp, but we need to
begin to think differently—to change our direction
of thinking. This world's standards and laws are
different from Heaven's, so we need to replace the
way this world has taught us to think with the way
Christ thinks. The world says take; Christ says give.

The world says judgment; Christ says mercy. Jesus taught that the poor in spirit are blessed; this stands in stark contrast to the world's standards. Paul calls us "ambassadors" of Jesus. As ambassadors we are not under the laws of the kingdom in which we are ambassadors. We remain under the laws of the kingdom in which we are citizens. Since our citizenship is in heaven, let us begin to think differently from the way this world does, and as we do we will begin to see that the kingdom of heaven is within our grasp here on earth.

Day 13

"Therefore everyone who hears these words of mine
and acts on them, may be compared to a wise man
who built his house on the rock. And the rain fell,
and the floods came, and the winds blew and
slammed against the house; and yet it did not fall,
for it had been founded on the rock. Everyone who
hears these words of Mine and does not act on
them, will be like a foolish man who built his house
on the sand. The rain fell, and the floods came, and
the winds blew and slammed against that house, and
it fell—and great was its fall." Matthew 7:24-27

Jesus describes for us in this parable two important
aspects of the Christian life. The first is that the
storm hits both houses. And it hits them with the
same intensity. Jesus is telling us that life with
Christ is not a shield from adversity. All will face
storms in life. The second aspect of what Jesus is
saying to us is this: it's impossible to withstand the

storms in life without Him. Eventually our house will fall if Christ is not our foundation. But He promises us that if we make Him our foundation, He will not let the storms in life destroy us. Our foundation will not fail. And in a life where storms can arise often, that promise certainly is comforting.

Day 14

"Though He slay me, I will hope in Him."
Job 13:15a
The end of a matter is better than its beginning.
Ecclesiastes 7:8a

I believe these two verses go hand in hand, and I
can find no better example of this than in the death
of Jesus. As the disciples sat bewildered at the death
of their Lord, God was working something that
would be the single most important event in
mankind. The horror of Christ's death would be
replaced by the eternal joy of His resurrection. Had
the disciples known this, they would have realized
that the hope found in Jesus transcends even death.
Job understood this, although he may not have
understood all of God's dealings with him. He knew
that not even death could conquer the hope that is

found in Jesus. Even when things are at their bleakest, when it seems God is nowhere to be found, for those who hope in Him God will make the end of the matter far better than its beginning. May we take comfort in this truth and never lose our hope in Him.

Day 15

Then He said to me, "Son of man, stand on your feet that I may speak with you!" As He spoke to me the Spirit entered me and set me on my feet; and I heard Him speaking to me.
Ezekiel 2:1-2

The Lord spoke to Ezekiel and called him to stand on his feet. Then as God spoke to Ezekiel, He filled him with His Spirit and set him on his feet. Notice that when God called Ezekiel to his feet, He empowered Ezekiel by His Spirit to accomplish that which He called Ezekiel to do. When God calls us to do something, we can be sure He will be faithful to supply all we need in order to accomplish it. And what do we need to answer God's calling? We need His Spirit. By His Spirit He will lift us and set us on our feet. And though the task He asks us to complete may be hard, He will be faithful to supply all our needs. This is such an encouraging picture of how God deals with His children.

Day 16

Though the fig tree should not blossom, and there
be no fruit on the vines, though the yield of the
olive should fail, and the fields produce no food,
though the flock should be cut off from the fold and
there be no cattle in the stalls, yet I will exult in the
LORD, I will rejoice in the God of my salvation. The
Lord GOD is my strength.
Habakkuk 3:17-19a

Habakkuk was living in a time of distress. From his
perspective it seemed as though the wicked were
prospering, while the righteous were struggling. But
in the midst of barrenness, God brought His eternal
perspective to Habakkuk. He would not forsake His
children, and Habakkuk knew that even when times
seemed especially hard, the Lord would provide for,
strengthen, and comfort those who call on His
name. With this perspective, Habakkuk could

confidently say in spite of the circumstances

surrounding him, "I will rejoice in the LORD, I will

joy in the God of my salvation."

Day 17

"Truly, truly, I say to you, unless a grain of wheat falls into the earth and dies, it remains alone; but if it dies, it bears much fruit."
John 12:24

From the beginning of creation God has been showing us the miracle of life resulting from death. Even in the most basic principles of agriculture, life comes from the dead seed. It is sobering to realize that God knew the suffering He would eventually have to go through on earth. Jesus knew that He would have to die in order that we might live. But He also knew that the life after death would be far greater than the life before death. This spiritual principle is not only true with salvation, but also in everyday life. As we surrender our lives to Christ, He raises us up in His new life and gives us victory in our day-to-day lives. Whatever issues arise in life, the Lord asks us to lay them at His feet. When we do, we find that He is more than sufficient to handle them and satisfy our every need.

Day 18

While He was saying these things to them, a
synagogue official came and bowed down before
Him, and said, "My daughter has just died; but
come and lay Your hand on her and she will live."
Matthew 9:18

By bowing at Jesus's feet and publicly declaring his
faith in Him, the synagogue official was risking his
reputation, his social status, his religious status, and
even his own livelihood. He would likely be
excommunicated from the synagogue for such a
declaration. But his love for his daughter and his
desire for her to live far outweighed anything else.
Faced with this desperate circumstance, the decision
was easy. When he finally surrendered his pride and
gave up worrying about what others would think, he
not only had a personal encounter with the living
God but also no longer hindered his daughter from

being saved. He fell at Jesus's feet in realization

that salvation only comes from Him. Sometimes the

Lord will allow us to go through the valley of the

shadow of death for us to grow closer to Him, and

in the process He gives us a personal encounter with

our precious Savior. However dire our situation

may seem, we can confidently trust that Christ will

guide us through it.

Day 19

The LORD said to him, "What is that in your hand?"
And he said, "A staff." Then He said, "Throw it on
the ground." So he threw it on the ground, and it
became a serpent; and Moses fled from it. But the
LORD said to Moses, "Stretch out your hand and
grasp it by its tail"—so he stretched out his hand
and caught it, and it became a staff in his hand—
"that they may believe that the LORD, the God of
their fathers, the God of Abraham, the God of Isaac,
and the God of Jacob, has appeared to you."
Exodus 4:2-5

The staff represented to Moses his identity—what
he was and what he did. He was a shepherd of
flocks; that's what he knew, that's what he was
comfortable doing. But God asked him to lay it
down, to surrender it. The Lord asked Moses to give
up the identity he had made for himself and become
identified with God and His purpose. The staff

became a serpent so Moses could see what he was really holding on to. As long as Moses held on to his identity without surrendering himself to God, the thing he clutched, his staff, the very thing that God intended to use in his life, would eventually turn into his foe. But Moses obeyed the Lord and surrendered it, and when he did the Lord asked him to do an interesting thing: He asked Moses to pick it up again. Moses had to trust God, he had to have faith to grasp the serpent, and when he did it became a staff again. Moses's identity no longer was found in what he did; it was now firmly established in his relationship with God. That staff, when left unsurrendered had the potential to harm Moses, became the instrument the Lord would use to perform many miracles within the hand of Moses. Moses now carried the staff not as a shepherd of flocks, but as the shepherd of God's people. By surrendering himself completely he was able to have a relationship with God that few have ever experienced. What is the staff in our hands that the Lord is asking us to lay down? I pray we have courage like Moses to surrender it and watch as the Lord transforms it into an instrument to advance His kingdom.

Day 20

Be anxious for nothing, but in everything by prayer
and supplication, with thanksgiving, let your
requests be made known to God; and the peace of
God, which surpasses all understanding, will guard
your hearts and minds through Christ Jesus.
Philippians 4:6-7

Paul reminds us here that in an ever changing and
often uncertain world, one thing remains constant—
God's faithfulness. Whatever trials or difficulties
we face in life, Jesus has told us to bring them to
Him because He is more than capable of handling
them. Paul urges us to find our peace in Christ, not
in our circumstances. It's important for us to
remember that Christ is faithful in all things;
faithfulness is part of who He is. And in that
knowledge we can find a wealth of peace that is
ours for the taking.

Day 21

By this the love of God was manifested in us, that
God has sent His only begotten Son into the world
so that we might live through Him. In this is love,
not that we loved God, but that He loved us and sent
His Son to be the propitiation for our sins. Beloved,
if God so loved us, we also ought to love one
another.
1 John 4:9-11

When you look at Jesus's life and study what He

taught, contemplate the relationship he had with

others, and think about the acts He accomplished,

one can only logically conclude that He is the

manifestation of Love. No other figure in all of

history displayed the type of love for mankind that

Jesus did. Love may be mocked, ridiculed, laughed

at, or even denied, but it cannot be ignored. Love of

this great magnitude demands a response. When we

personally encounter this Love we all must make a choice: for or against. How we live our lives is directly related to our response to this Love. The lie of the devil is that voicing our encounter with Jesus might be offensive to some, and so we should not do it. The offense comes not from Love, but rather from the denial of it. Let them be offended, but let not Love be silent in our lives.

Day 22

Rejoice in the Lord always; again I will say, rejoice!
Philippians 4:4

When Paul wrote these words he was imprisoned
and in a seemingly hopeless situation. Yet he
continually rejoiced. The reality is that even in the
direst circumstances we have something to be
thankful for. This isn't to minimize or trivialize
anyone's hardships, and I'm not trying to feign
naivety at the reality of the pain that is out there. It's
more an attempt at living in the reality of the hope
that is found in Jesus—that even on our worst day
we can realize God loves us and is with us in the
midst of the trial. He is our comforter. Greater still
is the fact that He is a good God with only good
intentions. Even though that truth might not
resonate in our present reality, His purpose will be

accomplished. We can trust His purpose is good because He is a good God. When we're tempted to doubt that fact we need only remember the cross; the cross certainly is something to rejoice in.

Day 23

When it was evening, the boat was in the middle of the sea, and He was alone on the land. Seeing them straining at the oars, for the wind was against them, at about the fourth watch of the night He came to them, walking on the sea; and He intended to pass by them. But when they saw Him walking on the sea, they supposed that it was a ghost, and cried out; for they all saw Him and were terrified. But immediately He spoke to them, "Take courage; it is I, do not be afraid."
Mark 6:47-50

When God calls us to something, it doesn't necessarily mean smooth sailing. When the disciples arrived on the other side of the sea, there was a tremendous amount of ministry that took place. One could even call it a revival (Mark 6:54-56). But before that could take place, the disciples had to weather the storm that lay between them and that time of breakthrough. When we purpose in our heart to follow the Lord, we can expect to be met with storms along the way. But it is key to remember that we cannot accomplish in the flesh what God has called us to; we must rely on His Spirit to accomplish it. To try to accomplish His purposes in our own power is akin to trying to row a boat through a storm—you will get nowhere and eventually become exhausted. The other mistake the disciples made was forgetting to look for Jesus in the midst of their storm. We often pray and plead for the storm to pass, but we forget to look for Jesus's comforting presence in the midst of the storm. It's His presence that enables us to walk upon the waves of the storm, and it's His presence that is capable of silencing the storm altogether.

Day 24

But an hour is coming, and now is, when the true
worshipers will worship the Father in spirit and
truth; for such people the Father *seeks* to be His
worshipers.
John 4:23

The term that is used here for the word "seeks" can
also be translated as "hunts." The Lord literally
hunts us; He pursues us in hopes that we will enter
into the relationship He originally intended to have
with us in the Garden of Eden. Before we sinned,
Adam and Eve enjoyed daily life in God's presence.
They talked with Him, they lived with Him, and
they did life with Him. Ever since sin entered the
world and created a barrier between God and us, He
has been actively pursuing us in order to regain that
intimacy with us again. As a hunter stalks his prey,
our Creator desperately seeks us in order to bless us.

Second Chronicles 16:9 says, "For the eyes of the LORD move to and fro throughout the earth that He may strongly support those whose heart is completely His." It is a pursuit initiated by God as a result of His overwhelming love for us. The Lord will stop at nothing to bring us back into an intimate relationship with Himself.

Day 25

"For which one of you, when he wants to build a tower, does not first sit down and calculate the cost to see if he has enough to complete it?"
Luke 14:28

Many don't realize that discipleship comes with a warning. Discipleship is not merely adherence to a doctrine or devotion to a lifestyle; it is relational, it is personal. Jesus was God in human form, so He had all the resources imaginable. If He wanted He could have simply hired people to spread His message of love and forgiveness, but what good would that do? Change doesn't happen unless it takes root in the inner man where it becomes personal and has the opportunity to grow and blossom. This is why Jesus invested in His disciples. I don't believe God simply wants

converts; He wants sons and daughters. It's
astounding to me that the God of the universe calls
us His children and desires to have that sort of
intimate, family relationship with us. "See how
great a love the Father has bestowed on us, that we
should be called children of God; and such we are"
(1 John 3:1a). When it is personal, then discipleship
is real.

Day 26

It happened that while Jesus was praying in a
certain place, after He had finished, one of His
disciples said to Him, "Lord, teach us to pray just as
John also taught his disciples." And He said to
them, "When you pray, say…"
Luke 11:1-2a

Prayer is our gateway to intimacy. I find it
interesting that during Jesus's earthly ministry He
explicitly taught and instructed the disciples on
prayer. It's recorded for us that He gave the
disciples specific instructions on this matter. We
aren't told if He gave the disciples specific
instructions on how to speak in tongues or on how
to prophecy, but we are deliberately given
instructions to pray and then given an example of
how to pray. Jesus doesn't tell the disciples, "*If* you
pray." He says, "*When* you pray." Prayer is not

optional in the disciples' life. Remember in the account of Jesus overturning the money changers' tables in front of the temple, one of His outcries was that the temple was not being used for its intended purpose. He lamented, "It is written, 'My house shall be called a house of prayer'" (Matthew 21:13). If prayer is this important to Jesus, then it should hold the same importance in our lives.

Day 27

"God created man in His own image, in the image
of God He created him; male and female He created
them. God blessed them; and God said to them…"
Genesis 1:27-28a

Notice in the account of the creation of man, the
first thing God did was to bless man and converse
with him. His first order of business with us upon
our creation was not only to bless us, but also to
start a dialogue with us. This should immediately
tell us two things. The first is that God desires to
bless us; His intentions toward us are good ones. He
wants what's best for us (Jeremiah 29:11). The
second thing it tells us is that God has always
intended for us to have a personal relationship with
Him. I'm convinced the only true way to know
someone is to spend time with that person, to

interact with them, to engage and be engaged by them. I can read a man's autobiography and know everything that happened in the life of that person, but still be a complete stranger to him. The only way to get to know Christ is to spend time with Him, to talk to Him, to learn His voice, and to get familiar with His personality. God is, and has always been, a personal God; He wants to talk with us. He gives us His Spirit so that we will never be apart from Him. He earnestly desires a relationship with each one of us and will go to every extreme to give us the opportunity to experience that relationship with Him. From the moment He made us He has been speaking to us, pursuing us with a love so passionate that no human can accurately articulate it completely.

Day 28

Now may the God of hope fill you with all joy and peace in believing, so that you will abound in hope by the power of the Holy Spirit.
Romans 15:13

I once heard that hope is the oxygen to the human soul. I believe this statement. We are designed to hope. It is written into our DNA. If we are made in the image of God, then we are certainly made to hope; after all, it is impossible to be in the presence of God and not be overwhelmed with hope. His presence demands it. His very nature is hope manifested. When He created us, He created us to hope in Him, to experience a degree of expectation in His goodness. After all, He is good and whatever He does is good, so however He interacts in our lives we can rest assured that it is good. This reality is how the disciples were able to sing while imprisoned; it is how people are able to endure the unthinkable and still praise God. And it is how we are meant to face each circumstance in our lives, whether good or bad. The reality is that God is good, and in Him is an abyss of hope that can't be fathomed.

Day 29

Abraham said to his young men, "Stay here with the
donkey, and I and the lad will go over there;
and *we* will worship and return to you."
Genesis 22:5

What happens when God is silent? What do you do?

Genesis 22 is yet another example of Abraham's

trust in God's character. Abraham had an amazing

characteristic of believing God regardless of his

circumstances. When God asked Abraham to leave

his homeland, Abraham listened and believed God

would guide him. When God told him he was going

to have a child even though he was ninety-nine

years old, Abraham believed Him. Even when God

asked Abraham to do something that was

completely contrary to the nature and character of

God, Abraham obeyed. But he didn't just obey; he

obeyed with a confidence that God could not deny Himself. He obeyed with a faithful assurance that God could not do something that was contradictory to His character. Even though God had asked him to offer Isaac, Abraham was certain that Isaac would return from the sacrifice with him. Abraham's response in verse five is evidence that he knew Isaac would return with him, even if that meant God would have to raise him from the dead. Abraham was so confident in God he never questioned Him even when his circumstances seemed to contradict God's very nature.

Day 30

"Whoever does not carry his own cross and come after Me cannot be My disciple."

Luke 14:27

It's interesting to me to think about what the cross must have meant to those to whom Jesus was speaking. It was a symbol of a humiliating, criminal, and painful death. So what Jesus said wasn't exactly the thing to say in order to garner a following among the listeners. Why did Jesus say that then? Jesus goes on to say, "…none of you can be My disciple who does not give up all his own possessions" (Luke 14:33). Again, not exactly the type of thing you want to say if you are looking to gain a following, which obviously Jesus didn't seem too concerned about. But still, why would He state such a thing? When I think of the cross, I believe it represents much more than sacrifice. I believe what actually place when Jesus willingly chose the cross was much more than a sacrifice. It was a complete identification with and understanding of the Father's great plan. It was trust in His plan, trust in the results of obedience. It was the King of all creation removing all of His justly due glory, His justly due honor, even His own rights. It was the ability to see success from Heaven's standpoint. At one point Jesus had thousands of followers; at the end of His earthly life even His eleven closest friends deserted Him. If you were to judge His life from a worldly standpoint, it would be hard to call it a success. Yet His obedience still echoes through all eternity. His obedience changed the course of this world and continues to do so even today. So I think that perhaps what Jesus was getting at was that if we are to truly be successful in this life, it is going

to require us to view success from a different

perspective—from a heavenly one.

Made in the USA
San Bernardino, CA
09 August 2017